The
SEASONS

Troll Associates

The
SEASONS

by Francene Sabin

Illustrated by Ray Burns

Troll Associates

Library of Congress Cataloging in Publication Data

Sabin, Francene.
    Seasons.

    Summary: Explains why there are four seasons in the
temperate zones and none at the equator and the Poles,
and mentions some of nature's signs that the seasons are
changing.
        1. Seasons—Juvenile literature.   [1. Seasons]
I. Burns, Raymond, 1924-   ill.   II. Title.
QB631.S23   1985   574.5'43   84-2713
ISBN 0-8167-0308-6 (lib. bdg.)
ISBN 0-8167-0309-4 (pbk.)

Icy winds rattle the bare branches of trees. Snow glistens on the ground. The days are short; the nights are long. Winter is here.

But time passes, and soon the buds on the trees grow fat, open, and send out tiny green shoots. Blades of grass poke through the ground, and birds start building their nests. The days grow longer and warmer. Spring is here.

Now flowers brighten the landscape. Insects buzz and hum. The days are long and hot. Summer is here.

Then one morning there is a chill mist over the ground. The tree leaves turn red, brown, orange, and yellow. Soon they drop to the ground. The days are growing short again. Autumn is here.

Winter, spring, summer, autumn. These are the four seasons that make up our year. But *why* are there seasons? Because of the relationship of our planet Earth to the sun. The Earth travels around the sun in a path called an orbit. This orbit takes a little more than 365 days, which is the length of time we call a year. The Earth takes one year to make a full orbit of the sun.

9

As the Earth orbits the sun, it also spins on its axis. The axis is an imaginary line that runs through the Earth from the North Pole to the South Pole. The rotation of the Earth on its axis causes day and night.

The Earth's axis is not straight up and down. It is tilted slightly. The seasons of the year are caused by the tilt of the Earth's axis as the Earth travels in its orbit around the sun. When the North Pole is tilted closest to the sun, the days are longer in the northern half of the Earth. It is summer in that part of the world.

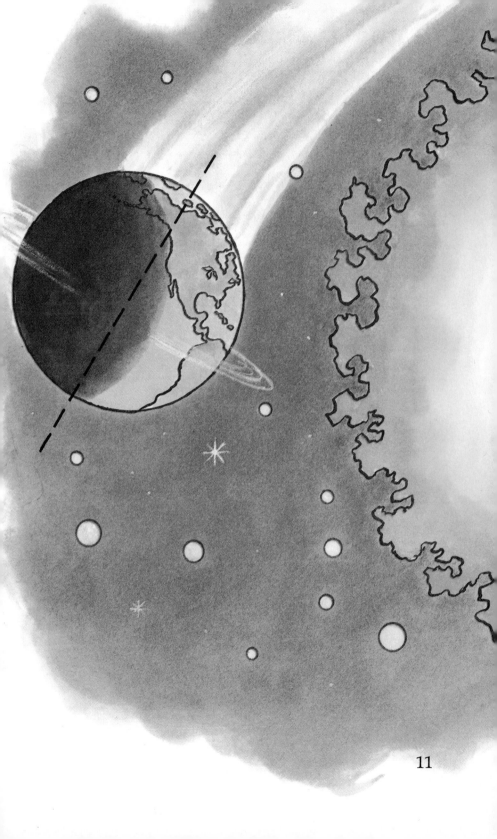

But the Earth continues moving in its orbit. After three months, the North and South Poles are the same distance from the sun. The hours of daylight and darkness are equal. It is the beginning of autumn in the northern part of the world.

After three more months, the Earth has moved to the part of its orbit in which the North Pole is tilted farthest from the sun.

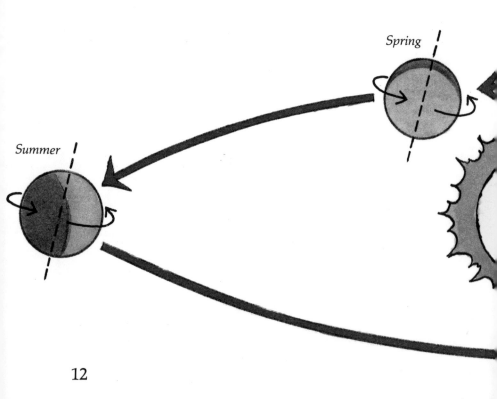

Now the days are short in the northern part of the world. It is winter there.

After three more months have passed, the North and South Poles are again the same distance from the sun. Daylight and darkness hours are again of equal length. It is the first day of spring in the northern part of the world. And three months later, it will be summer once again.

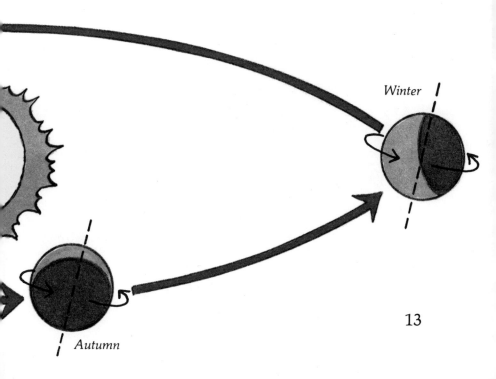

Winter

Autumn

13

At the fattest part of the Earth, halfway between the North Pole and the South Pole, is the equator. The equator is an imaginary line around the middle of our planet.

Everything between the North Pole and the equator is in the Northern Hemisphere. The word *hemisphere* means "half of a ball." Everything between the South Pole and the equator is in the Southern Hemisphere.

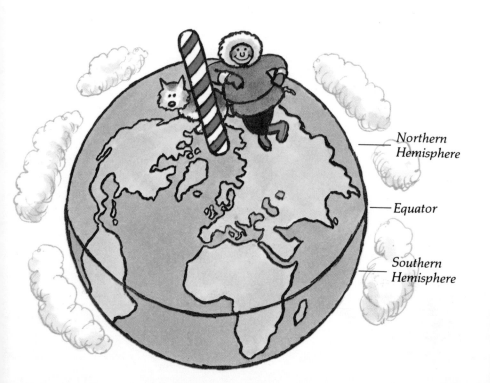

Northern Hemisphere

Equator

Southern Hemisphere

In the area near the equator, the climate is hot throughout the year. The seasons don't bring much change in temperature there. At the North and South Poles, it is always very cold. The seasons don't bring much change in temperature to those regions either. But in the parts of the Earth between the Poles and the equator, the seasons bring noticeable changes.

The seasons in the Northern and Southern Hemispheres are reversed. This means that when the Northern Hemisphere has summer, the Southern Hemisphere is having winter. And when it is winter in the Northern Hemisphere, it is summer in the Southern Hemisphere.

16

In the Northern Hemisphere, the shortest day of the year occurs about December 22. This is called the winter solstice. On this day the North Pole is tilted farthest from the sun. This is the first day of winter. From this day on, the daylight hours will last a minute or two longer, and the hours of darkness will be a minute or two shorter.

On the day of the winter solstice, the sun rides low in the sky. Even at noon, the sun casts long shadows. Then, as the days grow longer, the sun rides higher and casts a shorter noontime shadow.

On about March 22, when the North and South Poles are the same distance from the sun, the hours of daylight and darkness are the same length. Each is twelve hours long. This day is called the spring equinox.

The longest day of the year is about June 22. It is called the summer solstice. On this day the North Pole is closer to the sun than on any other day of the year. The noon sun is at its highest point—so high that it seems to be right over your head.

After the summer solstice, the days begin to grow shorter. About September 22 there are exactly twelve hours of daylight and twelve hours of night. This is the autumn equinox. From now on, the days will grow shorter than the nights until about December 22, the day of the winter solstice.

We also call December 22 the first day of winter. But that doesn't mean there is a sharp change in the weather on that day. Winter weather comes on little by little. So do the changes that mark the other seasons.

Living things are affected by the change of seasons. Most plants cannot produce new leaves, flowers, and fruit all year long. Many kinds of birds cannot live in cold climates and must migrate to warm places before winter comes.

Even people must change the way they live as the seasons change. We wear warmer clothing and heat our homes in the winter. Farmers plant crops in the spring and harvest them in the summer and fall.

People keep track of the changing seasons with calendars. The calendar tells the farmer when to plant and when to harvest. It tells store owners when to put summer clothing on display, and it tells you when school will end and vacation begin.

Plants and animals can't use a calendar. So how do they know when one season is changing into another? They tell by how long daylight lasts and by the warmth of the temperature. In other words, the sun is their calendar. As the days grow shorter and cooler in autumn, the change of weather is a message to the animals and plants that winter is coming.

Squirrels bury acorns. Chipmunks store seeds and nuts in underground burrows. Many birds start their long flights to the south. Some rabbits' coats turn from brown to white and grow thicker. Some insects lay eggs that will hatch in spring. Other insects go underground or into trees or under rocks.

Autumn weather signals plants to shed their leaves. It also tells plants not to send out new roots. Now they must save their energy. The cold winter months are coming.

What do plants do during the short, frigid days of winter? They just try to survive. And for all those that do, the rewards come with the first signs of spring.

But even before the days are warm and before the spring equinox arrives, some of nature's early risers wake up. The crocus and the snowdrop do not need many hours of sunlight or warmth to bloom. Other plants will not flower until April or May or later. Every kind of plant has its own daylight calendar.

The same is true for birds and animals and insects. Robins return from the far south when there are about twelve hours of daylight. Spring also brings back the ducks and geese that flew south for the winter. It is time for chipmunks to pop out of their burrows, for insect eggs to hatch, for

worms to come up from underground tunnels. It is time for birds to lay eggs, for animals to bear young, for deer to sprout new antlers, and for rabbits' coats to turn from white to brown.

The heat and long days of summer tell the plants to bloom and grow, to bear fruit, to send out roots. It is the time for animals to grow fat, to raise their young, and to enjoy the riches of the land.

For soon the days will grow cool and short once more. Night's darkness will grow longer as autumn comes on. And soon again it will be winter. The never-ending circle of change we call the seasons spins on and on and on....